Discovering
the Reality of God

JAMES B. POLSON

WESTBOW
PRESS®
A DIVISION OF THOMAS NELSON
& ZONDERVAN

Portions of this book were published previously under the title *Can a Skeptic Believe in God? My Story* (Nashville: Elm Hill, 2019).

This book is a work of non-fiction. Unless otherwise noted, the author and the publisher make no explicit guarantees as to the accuracy of the information contained in this book and in some cases, names of people and places have been altered to protect their privacy.

WestBow Press books may be ordered through booksellers or by contacting:

WestBow Press
A Division of Thomas Nelson & Zondervan
1663 Liberty Drive
Bloomington, IN 47403
www.westbowpress.com
844-714-3454

Scripture quotations are taken from the Holy Bible, King James Version.

ISBN: 979-8-3850-1306-7 (sc)
ISBN: 979-8-3850-1307-4 (e)

Library of Congress Control Number: 2023922242

Print information available on the last page.

WestBow Press rev. date: 2/2/2024

To my wonderful wife,
NANCY

CONTENTS

CHAPTER ONE

Searching for Truth

INTRODUCTION

In this book, I recount my journey in search of truth about God, heaven, and hell; and I am writing it with the earnest desire that it will help you understand how you can know where you will spend eternity before you ever face your own death. Perhaps you are skeptical about whether it is possible to know anything at all about life beyond the grave, and you are not interested in the wild claims of fanatics or encounters with religious zealots. I understand. I also was a skeptic who thought that God, heaven, and hell likely did not exist outside of one's imagination.

I was satisfied with that view of things until I was involved in a car accident that made me realize that death can happen at any time. And what if I was wrong about heaven and hell? What if they really do exist? Where would I be? The more I dwelled on it, the more I was driven by the thought that even if there was only a small fraction of a chance that I could spend eternity in hell, the stakes were high enough that I would be foolish not to check it out before it was too late to do anything about it. So I ventured forth to see if I could discover any truth about the existence of God, heaven, and hell.

Contrary to my expectations, I found that it can be proven that God is alive, and that the Bible, which speaks about heaven and hell, is His communication to humankind. And it is vitally important that people know about these truths. So I am writing this book to explain to you what I found and how, I believe, the providence of God led me to it. I have also included chapters on how you can take advantage of the blessings that only God can provide. If you would like to benefit from what I discovered, please read on.

My father was a good role model for seeking truth. Although encumbered with the imperfections of being human, he was known as an honest man among his family and friends. In addition, he was well-read and had a high regard for science, education, and the arts. He was a factory worker in my early years, but by working during the day and attending night school at the University of Kansas City, he earned a degree in chemistry and became a chemical engineer. My mother was a talented artist who added beauty to our modest home with the sketches and paintings she hung on the walls.

My parents sought the truth about God by regularly attending church, but for me, church was a mixed blessing. The pastor was as sincere and devoted as they come, and he used the Bible when he preached. Many people seemed to gain biblical insights from his messages, but I did not. For a long time, I was confused about what one must do to escape punishment in hell for one's sins. However, by the time I entered college, I was reading the Bible for myself and praying to God for guidance. I think that by that time, I had placed my faith in Jesus alone for the forgiveness of my sins, but my understanding was shallow. When some acquaintances asked me how I knew there was a God and how I knew Jesus was the Son of God, I drew a blank. I simply said, "You gotta have faith," as though having faith supported by nothing was God's test of your character. That answer did not satisfy my acquaintances, nor did it satisfy me; and I guess I knew in the back of my mind that my theological understanding was a house of cards constructed on thin air.

In 1959, I married Nancy Keith, a lovely young lady who had dedicated her life to the Lord. We planned to build a home together that honored God. When we got married, she was in nurses' training, and after graduation, she worked in various hospitals as a registered nurse, giving comfort and healing to many patients. At the time that this manuscript was being prepared, Nancy and I celebrated our sixty-fourth wedding anniversary. She has been a wonderful wife and a faithful friend to me all through the years, even during my darkest hours.

After I graduated from college in 1961, I volunteered for service in the US Army. During active duty, my perspective on life changed dramatically. I was separated from Christian friends, did not attend church, quit reading my Bible, and quit praying; and over time, my faith in God dried up. By the time I was released from active duty, I was no longer interested in spiritual things. My new focus was building a career in the biomedical sciences.

To pursue that goal, I enrolled in graduate school at the University of Missouri, where I earned a PhD in pharmacology. After two years of postdoctoral training at the University of Minnesota, I joined the faculty of the University of South Florida, College of Medicine, where I taught and conducted research in the field of biochemical pharmacology for the next thirty-three years.

It was when I was about twenty-five years old that I turned my back on the things of God completely. After that, I seldom thought of or spoke of God at all, except to scoff at people who believed in Him. Outside of my need to live up to professional standards to keep my career intact, I had little regard for the moral laws of God or humankind. My wife, on the other hand, never lost her faith or her faithfulness. Although we had not attended church for years, she continued to pray. Her prayer for me was that God would do something to bring me back in line since she was convinced that I was His child. I believe God answered her prayer on June 1, 1977, when I was in a car accident.

On that date, a young woman drove her rental car past a stop sign and plowed it into the driver's side of my Dodge Dart, spinning it into a utility pole. I was injured. Suddenly, I found myself supine in an ambulance speeding toward an ER. As a paramedic hovered over me, I thought, *What if I am dying? What if I am about to be hurled toward the abyss of eternity with no time to prepare? This is no joke!* I didn't know what was happening to me. I didn't know whether I would recover and be OK, whether I was about to swoon into the blackness of everlasting sleep, or whether I was about to be swallowed up by the terrors of hell. And frantic thoughts racing through my mind did nothing to help. I was scared!

Once the crisis was over and I was recovering from my injuries, I did not forget my excruciating experience. I knew that someday I would face death again, and sooner or later, it would be for real. I vowed to do everything in my power to at least try to prepare for death before it came around again. But how does one prepare for such a thing? I thought that, on the outside chance that God does exist somewhere, I should seek His help. So I closed my eyes and uttered a prayer. *God, if You exist, please help me find You.* Then I began my inquiry by giving God's existence some serious thought.

A GLIMMER OF HOPE

My line of reasoning led to three unexpected conclusions.

First, biomedical science and the theory of evolution cannot explain the existence of my thoughts, will, and emotions. There is no reason to believe that a simple chemical or physical reaction is aware of its own existence. If our bodies and brains are merely the products of complex combinations of chemical and physical reactions, where did my self-awareness come from? Even the artificial intelligence of our time is not alive and aware of its own existence. It does not possess a soul that can be stirred by such things as love, joy, sorrow, and pain. And if I do not know where this immaterial part of my being comes from, how do I know what happens to it when I die? And isn't it possible that somewhere, somehow, a greater self-awareness exists that is not detectable or explainable by science? In other words, as far as I know as a scientist, it is possible that a living God does exist.

Second, if there is a God, He would probably try to communicate with His creation. Since written language is the most reliable and long-lasting means of communication between people, it seemed logical that if God were to try to communicate with humankind, written language would be involved. For a written work to be a communication from God to humankind, it logically would have to be (1) something that has been available to many people throughout the ages and (2) something that is widely proclaimed to be the Word of God. Do we know of any written works that meet these criteria? The Bible and the Koran come to mind. Just because they meet these criteria does not prove that they came from God, but it does suggest that they are worthy of further study.

Third, God might want to visit humankind. But what form would He take to do so? Most likely He would take on the form of a human being in order to facilitate communication between Himself and people. However, He would also want to set Himself apart from other human beings. How would He do that? By appearance? By stature? By longevity? What about allowing Himself to be put to death in public and then coming back from the dead? That would do it. But that's what Jesus did. Oh wow, that seems like real evidence that Jesus is God in human form. Then I remembered Jesus's claim of divinity and how His disciples endured torture and gave up their lives rather than recant their testimony that He had risen from the dead.

I also knew that Jesus had extremely high moral standards and denounced sin. But where did that leave me? I was a wretched sinner. Did this mean that I was about to be condemned to hell forever? Fear surged through me like a charge of electricity. I was afraid of the answer to that question, but I was desperate to know it. I blurted out, "God, … Jesus, … I am a wretched sinner, but I don't want to be cast into hell. Is there a chance for me to escape that fate? Is there a chance for me?"

As I ended my desperate cry for help, the Bible verse John 3:16 came to mind for the first time since my youth. The words were like a life preserver flung to a drowning man. "For God so loved the world, that he gave his only begotten Son, that whosoever believeth in him should not perish, but have everlasting life."

I said, "Lord, I don't know for sure how to believe, and I am a skeptic by nature and by training. I'm not settled in my mind that You are truly God. But the best way I know how, I am making a commitment right now. I'm placing my eternal destiny in Your hands. Please forgive my sins. Please save me. I am depending on You."

A FAITHFUL BIBLE TEACHER

Over the weeks that followed that desperate prayer, I longed to know more about God. I turned to the Bible, which consists of the Old and New Testaments. I found a copy of the New Testament in a modern translation and read it through. To my chagrin, it raised many questions I couldn't answer, and that fueled many doubts. So I prayed that God would lead me to a faithful Bible teacher. I didn't care whether the teacher was a Jewish rabbi, a Catholic priest, a Baptist preacher, or a hippie with a Bible in his lap. All I cared about was that he or she would know the Bible well, and be able to explain it. Most of all, I prayed that the teacher could show me verses that communicate clearly what one must do to escape hellfire and be admitted into heaven. I wanted to know for the sake of my family as well as myself. I wanted Nancy and my two children to know the truth about God.

I sought out a church of the same denomination I was raised in and attended a Sunday morning service in hopes of finding a faithful Bible teacher. The minister was very self-confident and forceful in his delivery. But he was not a good Bible teacher. I could not get out of there fast enough. The last thing that I wanted was to contend with an incompetent preacher, who was interested in entangling my family in his programs. I realized that I needed God's help to keep from being led astray. My prayers intensified.

I prayed for weeks, and the weeks turned into months. Soon it was November 1977. I was in the living room of my house praying in the wee hours of the morning. I was pleading with the Lord to lead me to a faithful Bible teacher soon. The TV was on. It was connected to a big antenna on the roof of my house that received signals from broadcast stations. It occurred to me that some stations feature ministers who give short devotionals at the end of each broadcast day. So I prayed, *Dear Lord, please let this be the answer to my prayers.* As soon as I ended my prayer, I walked down the hall to another room to get a pencil and paper to write down the name of the teacher I hoped the Lord would provide. Then I went back to the living room and sat down in front of the TV, all the time praying that this would be God's answer.

Soon a minister did appear on the screen, who began to explain from a worn, note-filled Bible what the scripture says about how to have eternal life. In the few minutes that he spoke, I was convinced that he was the kind of teacher I had been praying for. His presentation was straightforward and based entirely on the Bible, with clear verses to back up every assertion. I became so engrossed in the message that I forgot to get his name, but I did manage to write down the name of his church. It was Calvary Community Church. The next day, I told Nancy about it and told her that I didn't know whether the church was in Miami, Orlando, St. Pete, or even somewhere in California, but I wanted to go there to learn from that pastor. She said she knew exactly where it was, and it was located less than five miles from our house.

The man I heard was Dr. Hank Lindstrom. Soon my family and I were seated in his church. I learned from him that John 3:16 means exactly what it says, and there are many other verses that testify to the same truth. When John 3:16 says that "God so loved the world," it means that God loves everyone in the world, including me. When it says that "He gave His only begotten Son," it means that He sent His Son Jesus from heaven to pay for all the sins of the world by His death on the cross (1 Corinthians 1:3–4).

After Jesus was buried, He rose from the dead, demonstrating that He wasn't an ordinary man but the Son of God, who can be trusted to keep His promises. When John 3:16 says, "whosoever believeth in Him should not perish," it means that anyone who simply trusts Jesus to forgive their sins will never perish in hell. When it says, "but have everlasting life," it means that God makes it His personal responsibility to see to it that every believer in Jesus will live forever.

Pastor Lindstrom also showed me Ephesians 2:8–9, which says that we as believers are saved by grace (unmerited favor) through faith, and that salvation is not of ourselves, and it is not earned by our works. Therefore, it is a gift. Furthermore, eternal life is eternal. Jesus will never lose us (John 10:27–30), nor cast us out (John 6:37). When I applied these teachings to myself, I understood them to mean that, all I needed to do was to trust Jesus Christ alone as the Son of God who died for my sins and rose from the dead, and God would forgive me, and give me eternal life as a gift. Therefore, whether I had trusted Jesus as a young person in Missouri, or more recently in Florida, I would have been eternally saved from that moment on.

All of that sounds good, but I still had a problem. I was still a skeptic. I wanted to fully believe in God, Jesus, and the Bible, but try as I may, I could not shake free from the doubts. I had been trained as a biomedical scientist and had learned to be skeptical of claims that were not backed up by solid evidence. Where was the evidence that God is real and that what the Bible says is true? To me, convincing evidence was like water to a parched traveler in the desert. I desperately needed it. I longed for a Gibraltar of complete certainty, where I could find refuge from the angry waves of doubt that assailed me. In my desperation, I turned once again to God.

I didn't know what else to do but to ask God to provide the solid evidence I needed to bring peace to my troubled soul. So I formulated a prayer to lay before the throne of grace. My petition went something like this:

> Dear God, I know I have no right to doubt Your word, and I am ashamed to admit that I am such a skeptic. But I'm asking for Your help once again. Please provide the following:

1. Solid evidence, written into the pages of Your Bible, showing that it is supernaturally inspired by You and not merely the work of uninspired men.
2. Solid evidence that You actually exist as a supernatural being and are not merely the product of man's imagination.
3. Solid evidence that You are alive and active in the world today.
4. Please make your evidence something that I can witness with my own eyes and not merely see on the evening news or read about in an article. I don't care if You have to take me halfway

around the world. I want to experience Your evidence firsthand.

I pray in the name of our Lord Jesus Christ. Amen.

What kind of evidence could God possibly provide to meet my needs? Would He provide any at all?

GOD'S ANSWER TO MY SKEPTICISM

The answer came based on a simple fact. Only God knows the future far enough ahead of time, and in clear enough detail, to be able to write history centuries before it happens. An example of this is God's Old Testament prophecies concerning the nation of Israel.

First, when the Jewish people were about to enter the Promised Land for the first time, it was prophesied that the day would come when God would expel them from their land and scatter them among the nations.[1] It is written in the book of Deuteronomy, "And

---

[1] John F. Walvoord, *Every Prophecy of the Bible* (Colorado Springs: David C. Cook, 2011), 38.

it shall come to pass, that as the LORD rejoiced over you to do you good, and multiply you, so the LORD will rejoice over you to destroy you, and bring you to nought; and ye shall be plucked from off the land whither thou goest to possess it. And the LORD shall scatter thee among all people, from one end of the earth even unto the other" (Deuteronomy 28:63–64). The worldwide dispersion of the Jewish people that was thus predicted came about approximately fifteen centuries after this prophecy was written.

Second, the regathering of the Jewish people into the Promised Land from among the nations where the Lord had scattered them was foretold by several Old Testament prophets.[2] For example, Jeremiah records the words of the Lord in chapter 23 verses 7–8: "Therefore, behold, the days come, saith the LORD, that they shall no more say, The LORD liveth, which brought up the children of Israel out of the land of Egypt; But, The LORD liveth, which brought up and led the seed of the house of Israel out of the north country, and from all countries whither I had driven them; and they shall dwell in their own land."

---

[2] Walvoord, *Major Bible Prophecies* (Grand Rapids: Zondervan, 1991), 84–95.

Ezekiel 34 says in verses 11–14,

> For thus saith the Lord GOD; Behold, I,
> even I, will both search my sheep, and
> seek them out. As a shepherd seeketh out
> his flock in the day that he is among his
> sheep that are scattered; so will I seek
> out my sheep, and will deliver them out
> of all places where they have been scat-
> tered in the cloudy and dark day. And I
> will bring them out from the people, and
> gather them from the countries, and will
> bring them to their own land, and feed
> them upon the mountains of Israel by the
> rivers, and in all the inhabited places of
> the country. I will feed them in a good
> pasture, and upon the high mountains of
> Israel shall their fold be: there shall they
> lie in a good fold, and in a fat pasture shall
> they feed upon the mountains of Israel.

Note that it is the Lord God who said He will bring
these things to pass.

In addition, Ezekiel 37:1–14 gives a vision of a valley

of dry bones. In this vision, the bones represent the Jewish people, as good as dead, dispersed among the nations. Verse 12 says in part, "Thus saith the Lord GOD; Behold, O my people, I will open your graves and cause you to come up out of your graves, and bring you into the land of Israel." Thus, this vision also predicts the restoration of the Jewish people to their land. Note again that it is the Lord God who says He will cause this to happen.

In a related prophecy in Ezekiel 36, the Lord spoke to the mountains of Israel, telling them that the time will come when they will be inhabited and transformed by His people.

> But ye, O mountains of Israel, ye shall shoot forth your branches, and yield your fruit to my people of Israel; for they are at hand to come. For, behold, I am for you, and I will turn unto you, and ye shall be tilled and sown: And I will multiply men upon you, all the house of Israel, even all of it: and the cities shall be inhabited, and the wastes shall be builded: And I will multiply upon you man and beast; and

they shall increase and bring fruit: and I
will settle you after your old estates, and
will do better unto you than at your be-
ginnings: and ye shall know that I am the
LORD. (Ezekiel 36:8–11)

Again, it is the LORD who said He will bring about
this transformation.

The fulfillment of these prophecies had already
begun in the twentieth century.[3] In his book, *Israel
Rising*,[4] Doug Hershey documents the current transformation of the Promised Land with the help of pho-
tographs taken by Elise Theriault.

In March of 1978, barely four months after I first
set foot in Pastor Lindstrom's church, he led a tour of
Israel. He invited me to go, and I thought it would be
an interesting experience, but I did not see any more
significance to it at that time. I did not know the pre-
dictions of the Old Testament prophets until Pastor
Lindstrom explained them to us later.

On our journey, we entered the West Bank via a

---

[3] Walvoord, *Every Prophecy of the Bible*, 38.

[4] Doug Hershey, *Israel Rising* (New York: Kensington Publishing
Corp., 2018).

bridge over the Jordan River. My first visual evidence that, that prophecy was being fulfilled was the blue-and-white flag of Israel, with its Star of David, fluttering above a bunker at the west end of the bridge. As my eyes drank in that sight, an Israeli Phantom Jet flew by, barely three hundred feet above the desert floor, spreading thunder in its wake.

In Israel, I saw crops growing in fields that were once desolate. I saw Israeli tanks standing guard on the Golan Heights. I bought a leatherbound copy of the Hebrew Scriptures (Old Testament) from a Jewish shopkeeper in Jerusalem. I saw where the Knesset met and toured a building where portions of the Dead Sea Scrolls were housed. I saw men clad in black with prayer shawls, praying before the hallowed Western Wall, and I was dismayed by the horrors depicted in the Holocaust museum. I witnessed with my own eyes these and many more pieces of evidence that the Jewish people were repopulating and transforming the Promised Land. This was evidence that shows that the prophecies, written over twenty-five centuries ago, are being fulfilled today. This was evidence that proves that the Bible was authored by a supernatural, all-knowing God, and not merely by uninspired men.

This was evidence that God is alive and working in the world today. All points of my brash prayer to God for solid evidence were met completely.

You probably are not such a hardheaded skeptic that you need to travel halfway around the world to see evidence firsthand before you believe that these prophecies are being fulfilled. But I, in my insecurity, felt that I needed that kind of proof. That is what I prayed for, and I thank God that He was kind enough to give it to me.

SELECTED BIBLE PROPHECIES

Are there any other prophecies written in scripture that have been fulfilled? Yes, there are many. Some of them deal with the question of whether Jesus is really the Messiah (another word for Christ) promised by the Old Testament prophets. The Old Testament in the Christian Bible consists of the same writings as the Hebrew Scriptures of the Jewish faith. God inspired the writers of these scriptures to describe the features of the promised Messiah in order to help people identify Him when He arrived on planet Earth and to know in advance something about His mission. There are many such prophecies. I will quote only four that are especially meaningful to me.

First, Micah 5:2 says, "But thou, Beth-lehem Ephratah, though thou be little among the thousands of Judah, yet out of thee shall he come forth unto me that is to be ruler in Israel; whose goings forth have been from of old, from everlasting." This is a reference to the promised Messiah or the one who "is to be ruler in Israel." It speaks of His divine origin, as only God's origin has been "from everlasting." It says that the Messiah's "coming forth" (His appearance on earth) will be out of a little, insignificant town in Judaea named Bethlehem. Approximately seven hundred years after this prophecy was written, Jesus was born in the tiny town of Bethlehem in Judaea exactly as predicted (Luke 2:1–20).

Second, Daniel 9:24–26 tells us that it would be 483 years after a commandment is decreed to rebuild Jerusalem, until the coming of the Messiah. It says in verse 25, "Know therefore and understand, that from the going forth of the commandment to restore and to build Jerusalem unto the Messiah the Prince shall be seven weeks, and threescore and two weeks."

The weeks written about are weeks of years or seven-year periods. Thus, the prophecy calls for sixty-nine times seven, or 483 years, from the decree until the Messiah was to come to Israel. This prophecy was investigated by Sir Robert Anderson[5] and Alva J. McClain,[6] who reported that the specified commandment to rebuild Jerusalem was decreed by Artaxerxes in the twentieth year of his reign. The date of the decree was March 5, 444 BC. Using careful and detailed calculations, the date prophesied for the Messiah's arrival in Israel was found to be March 30, AD 33.[7] It was exactly on that date in history that Jesus entered Jerusalem, riding on the colt of a donkey, and offered Himself as King to Israel. Thus the prophecy was fulfilled with pinpoint accuracy.

The prophecy in Daniel 9 has another part to it. It predicted that the Messiah would be cut off (killed) before the city and sanctuary (temple) were destroyed.

---

[5] Sir Robert Anderson, *The Coming Prince* (Grand Rapids: Kregel Classics, 1957).

[6] Alva J. McClain, *Daniel's Prophecy of the 70 Weeks* (Winona Lake: BMH Books, 2007).

[7] J. Dwight Pentecost, "Daniel" In John F. Walvoord and Roy B. Zuck, ed., *The Bible Knowledge Commentary: Old Testament* (USA: Victor Books, 1988) 1323–1375.

Verse 26 says, "And after threescore and two weeks shall Messiah be cut off, but not for himself: and the people of the prince that shall come shall destroy the city and the sanctuary." The predicted destruction of the city of Jerusalem and the temple came about in AD 70. The death of the Messiah was before that (AD 33). Thus, that part of the prophecy was also fulfilled.

Third, the manner in which the Messiah would enter Jerusalem to offer Himself as King of Israel was prophesied in Zechariah 9:9, which says, "Rejoice greatly, O daughter of Zion; shout, O daughter of Jerusalem: behold thy King cometh unto thee: he is just, and having salvation; lowly, and riding upon an ass, and upon a colt the foal of an ass." This prophecy was fulfilled approximately five centuries later when Jesus rode into Jerusalem on the colt of a donkey to offer Himself as King (Matthew 21:1–11).

Fourth, Isaiah wrote that the Messiah would be rejected by the Jewish people. In this prophecy, the Messiah is referred to as "the arm of the LORD." Isaiah 53:1–4 says,

Who hath believed our report? And to whom is the arm of the LORD revealed?

For he shall grow up before him as a tender plant, and as a root out of dry ground: he hath no form nor comeliness; and when we shall see him, there is no beauty that we should desire him. He is despised and rejected of men; a man of sorrows, and acquainted with grief: and we hid as it were our faces from him; he was despised, and we esteemed him not. Surely he hath borne our griefs, and carried our sorrows: yet we did esteem him stricken, smitten of God, and afflicted.

In this passage, the prophet laments that his report about the Messiah would not be believed by his people and that the Messiah would be despised and rejected. Seven centuries after Isaiah wrote this prophecy, Jesus died on the cross at the hands of Gentile men after His rejection by the nation of Israel. Jesus was rejected despite His being the subject of fulfilled prophecies, despite bringing a message of love and salvation, despite performing miracles of healing and raising of the dead, and despite allowing Himself to be put to death in public and then rising from the dead three days later. Many, but not all, Jewish people still do not believe in Jesus as their Messiah today.

There is a special place in my heart for Jewish people for more than one reason. For one thing, many good Jewish friends and colleagues have had a strong positive influence on my personal and professional life. For another, I believe it is through the Jewish people that God chose to give the world His scriptures and His Messiah.

STATISTICAL ANALYSIS

In his book *The New Evidence That Demands a Verdict*,[8] Josh McDowell quotes sixty-one Old Testament prophecies about the Messiah that were fulfilled by Jesus when He came to earth. McDowell also cites Peter Stoner's report[9] of Hartzler's application of the principles of probability in order to demonstrate whether the fulfillment of the prophecies was merely by chance. He considered just eight of the fulfilled prophecies

---

[8] Josh McDowell, *The New Evidence That Demands a Verdict* (Nashville: Thomas Nelson Publishers, 1999), 164-202.

[9] Peter W. Stoner, *Science Speaks* (Chicago: Moody Press, 1963).

and found that the probability that all eight would be fulfilled merely by coincidence was one chance in 100 quadrillion (10 to the 17th power).

As an illustration, it was explained that it would be like taking 100 quadrillion silver dollars and layering them all over the state of Texas. They would form a layer two feet deep. Then mark one silver dollar and hide it somewhere among the mass of coins. Now blindfold a man and tell him he can travel as far as he wishes, but he must stop somewhere and pick up one silver dollar, claiming it to be the marked one. The chance that he would pick up the marked coin would be the same as the probability that the eight prophecies in question would be fulfilled by chance alone. In other words, it is extremely unlikely that the prophecies of the Bible were fulfilled merely by chance.

CONCLUSION

When I was a skeptic, praying desperately for some evidence to support the claim that the Bible was God's revelation to humankind and that Jesus was God in human form, I asked that God would write something into the scriptures to prove that they were authored by Him. Prophecies written in the Bible detailing history centuries before the events took place were the evidence that answered my prayers.

I summarized five prophecies in this book—all of which have been fulfilled centuries after they were written.

1. The regathering of the Jewish people into the land of Israel after nearly two thousand years of being scattered among the nations,
2. The predicted birthplace of Jesus in Bethlehem of Judaea,
3. The accurately predicted time of arrival of Jesus in Israel and His death before the destruction of Jerusalem and the temple,
4. The manner in which He entered Jerusalem to offer Himself as King of the Jews, and
5. The rejection of Jesus by Isaiah's people.

These are only five of the many prophecies and types written into the Old Testament that have been fulfilled. The probability is infinitesimally small that biblical prophecies have been fulfilled by chance alone. God did not despise my need to have evidence and reason to underpin my faith in Him. Rather, He graciously met my need, and for that, I am eternally grateful.

Thus, fulfilled prophecy was the breakthrough that dispelled my doubts and fears. That, coupled with forty-five years of studying the Bible, witnessing biblical principles in action, and witnessing spectacular answers to the prayers of ordinary people, has led me to a faith and an inner peace that I could only have dreamed about in my former days of godless living. Now I am at rest, believing in Jesus with all my heart.

What about you? Have you trusted the Lord Jesus Christ alone to forgive your sins and give you eternal life? It's vitally important that you do. Jesus is trustworthy. He made this promise to you: "Verily, verily, I say unto you, He that believeth on me hath everlasting life" (John 6:47).

CHAPTER TWO

How to Have Eternal Life (The Gospel)

INTRODUCTION

Eternal life is free.[10] You do not have to give up anything, pledge anything, or surrender anything. All you have to do is trust Jesus to keep His promise to forgive your sins and give you eternal life as a gift,

---

[10] J. B. Hixson, Rick Whitmire, and Roy B. Zuck, ed., *Freely by His Grace: Classical Grace Theology* (Duluth: Grace Gospel Press, 2012), 615pp.

and He will do it. It sounds simple, and it is, unless false teachers have gotten to you with redefined words or out-of-context scriptures, making it complicated. There are many false teachers and many perverted versions of the gospel in the world. The apostle Paul contended with these in his ministry. He wrote to the Galatians, "But though we, or an angel from heaven preach any other gospel unto you than that which we have preached unto you, let him be accursed. As we said before, so say I now again, If any man preach any other gospel unto you than that ye have received, let him be accursed" (Galatians 1:7–8).

The purpose of this chapter is to present Bible verses that bear on the issue of eternal salvation, and how to acquire it. These verses are presented with brief explanations as to their significance. The goal is to make the gospel clear so that you can understand how to be certain that you have eternal life through faith, and so that you can protect yourself from false teachers.

WE ARE ALL SINNERS

The Bible says, "For all have sinned, and come short of the glory of God" (Romans 3:23). Everybody, except Jesus, is born with a sin nature that we inherited from Adam. As a result, we all fall short of God's standard of righteousness in the things we say and do every day. We are all guilty of sin.

THE PAYMENT FOR SIN IS DEATH

The Bible says, "For the wages of sin is death" (Romans 6:23). Since we are all sinners, we are all under the curse of death. This includes the second death, which is eternal separation from God in a lake of fire. Revelation 20:13–14 gives a preview of what lies in store for sinners at the great white throne judgment: "And the sea gave up the dead which were in it; and death and hell delivered up the dead which were in them: and they were judged every man according to their works. And death and hell were cast into the lake of fire. This is the second death."

NO ONE GUILTY OF SIN
CAN ENTER HEAVEN

God loves you and would rather that you spend eternity in heaven than in hell. However, heaven is a perfect place, and no one guilty of sin can get in. Even if you were only guilty of telling one lie, it would keep you from entering heaven. Revelation 21:27 speaks to that. "And there shall in no wise enter into it any thing that defileth, neither whatsoever worketh abomination, or maketh a lie."

YOU CAN DO NOTHING ON
YOUR OWN TO PAY FOR SIN

The only payment for sin is death (Romans 6:23). Living a good life will not pay for sin. Attending church, giving to the poor, volunteering for charitable organizations, or being baptized in water—none of these things, as good as they are, will pay for one sin. And we cannot make ourselves righteous by our works. Isaiah 64:6 says, "But we are all as an unclean thing, and all our righteousnesses are as filthy rags;

and we all do fade as a leaf; and our iniquities, like the wind, have taken us away." We need a Savior.

JESUS PAID FOR YOUR SINS BY HIS DEATH

The good news is that God loves you. No matter who you are, and no matter what you may have done, or failed to do in your life, God loves you, and he sent His only begotten Son, Jesus, from heaven to pay for your sins by His death on the cross. Romans 5:8 says, "But God commendeth his love toward us in that, while we were yet sinners, Christ died for us."

The apostle Paul reminded the Corinthians of the gospel he preached to them as follows: "For I delivered unto you first of all that which I also received, how that Christ died for our sins according to the scriptures; And that he was buried, and that he rose again the third day according to the scriptures" (1 Corinthians 15:3–4). All your sins—past, present, and future—were paid for by Jesus's one-time sacrifice in AD 33.

Hebrews 10:12 says, "But this man, after he had

offered one sacrifice for sins for ever, sat down on the right hand of God."

Hebrews 10:14 says, "For by one offering he hath perfected for ever them that are sanctified."

ALL YOU MUST DO TO RECEIVE ETERNAL LIFE IS TO TRUST JESUS TO GIVE IT TO YOU

You do not need to surrender your life to Christ, make Jesus lord of your life,[11] promise to clean up your life, or perform good works. Now don't get me wrong—all those things are good, and, in their proper place, they are the right things to do. But they can never take away sin or give you eternal life. All you must do to receive eternal life is believe, trust, or rely upon Jesus to keep His promise to give it to you as a gift.

John 3:16–18 says, "For God so loved the world, that he gave his only begotten Son, that whosoever believeth in him should not perish, but have everlasting life. For God sent not his Son into the world

[11] Charles C. Bing, *Lordship Salvation: A Biblical Evaluation and Response* (USA: Xulon Press, 2010), 233pp.

to condemn the world, but that the world through him might be saved. He that believeth on him is not condemned; but he that believeth not is condemned already, because he hath not believed in the name of the only begotten Son of God."

Your faith must be in Jesus Christ alone—not Jesus Christ, plus something you would do. Ephesians 2:8–9 says, "For by grace are ye saved through faith; and that not of yourselves: it is the gift of God: Not of works, lest any man should boast." Titus 3:5 says, "Not by works of righteousness which we have done, but according to his mercy he saved us."

Eternal life is eternal. Once you are saved, you are always saved. Jesus addressed this issue, using sheep to represent believers, in John 10:27–30. He said, "My sheep hear my voice, and I know them, and they follow me: And I give unto them eternal life; and they shall never perish, neither shall any man pluck them out of my hand. My Father, which gave them me, is greater than all; and no man is able to pluck them out of my Father's hand. I and my Father are one."

Once you have placed your faith in Jesus, you will never come into condemnation. You will never be put on trial at God's great white throne judgment, where unbelievers will be cast into the lake of fire. Jesus said, "Verily, verily, I say unto you, He that heareth my word, and believeth on him that sent me, hath everlasting life, and shall not come into condemnation; but is passed from death unto life" (John 5:24).

Once you have placed your faith in Jesus, He gives you the righteousness you need to enter heaven: "For he hath made him to be sin for us, who knew no sin; that we might be made the righteousness of God in him" (2 Corinthians 5:21).

You may ask, "What prayer must I pray to receive eternal life?" You do not have to pray at all. God knows your thoughts, and He knows when you believe in Jesus as your Savior. However, if you would like to tell God that you are believing in Jesus, you might say a prayer that sounds like this:

Dear God in heaven,

I admit that I am a sinner. But I believe that You sent Your Son, Jesus Christ, from heaven to save sinners. I believe that Jesus paid for all of my sins by His death on the cross, and after He was buried, that

He rose from the dead. I'm trusting Jesus, and Him alone, to forgive my sins and give me eternal life as a gift. Thank you for your great salvation. I pray in Jesus's name. Amen.

AS A BELIEVER, YOU CAN KNOW THAT YOU HAVE ETERNAL LIFE

First John 5:13 says, "These things have I written unto you that believe on the name of the Son of God; that ye may know that ye have eternal life." The Bible is your written guarantee. Therefore, you can have total confidence that eternal life is yours forever.

CHAPTER THREE

Six Good Reasons to Serve God

INTRODUCTION

Eternal life is free, but serving God is not. Once you have placed your faith in Jesus as your Savior, you are guaranteed to live with Him forever, even if you never lift a finger to serve Him. But serving God requires sacrifice.

So why serve Him at all? There are many reasons, but in this chapter, I present only six, that I hope will help you decide to live a life of Christian service. These are:

1. because you love Him,
2. because it is your reasonable service,
3. because it gives your life greater significance,
4. because it provides a better quality of life,
5. because it lessens the severity of God's chastening, and
6. because it accumulates treasure in heaven.

BECAUSE YOU LOVE HIM

This is perhaps the most noble of the reasons presented in this chapter. Some of Jesus's words to his disciples are recorded in John 14. He said, "If ye love me, keep my commandments" (v. 15). "He that hath my commandments, and keepeth them, he it is that loveth me: and he that loveth me shall be loved of my Father, and I will love him, and will manifest myself to him" (v. 21). "If a man love me, he will keep my words: and my Father will love him, and we will come unto him, and make our abode with him" (v. 23). Therefore, serving God because you love Him is a good thing. And the Bible says that we love Him, because He first loved us (1 John 4:19.)

BECAUSE IT IS YOUR REASONABLE SERVICE

In Romans 12:1–2, the apostle Paul wrote, "I beseech you therefore, brethren, by the mercies of God, that ye present your bodies a living sacrifice, holy, acceptable unto God, which is your reasonable service. And be not conformed to this world: but be ye transformed by the renewing of your mind, that ye may prove what is that good, and acceptable, and perfect will of God."

The first eleven chapters of Romans tell of many mercies associated with God's great salvation. For example, Christ died for us (Romans 5:8), we are made righteous by faith (Romans 3:22, 4:5), we are justified and given peace with God by faith (Romans 5:1), we are given eternal life as a gift (Romans 6:23), we are delivered from the power of sin (Romans 6:1–13), we are given the Holy Spirit (Romans 8:9–11), and the

Holy Spirit makes intercession for us (Romans 8:26), to name a few.

Then in the opening verses of chapter 12, Paul refers to these mercies and argues that in view of them, the life of sacrificial service that he is pleading for is only reasonable. It is reasonable, indeed!

BECAUSE IT GIVES YOUR LIFE GREATER SIGNIFICANCE

Without a meaningful purpose, our lives on earth would lack significance. What meaningful purposes do we have in serving the Lord? You can probably think of several. What stands out in my mind is working together with Christ to save lost souls from hell.

When I contemplate the awfulness and suffocating torment of hell that will never ever end, it moves me to want to do something to save people from ending up there. That's the main reason I am writing this book. I pray that you will join us in the quest to save souls from hell. It's a quest that gives our lives on earth a superlatively meaningful purpose. It gives our lives greater significance.

BECAUSE IT PROVIDES A BETTER QUALITY OF LIFE

In Galatians 5:16–23, the works of the flesh are contrasted with the fruit of the Spirit. The works of the flesh are the consequences of choosing to live according to fleshly appetites. The fruit of the Spirit is the consequence of choosing to walk in the Spirit (live according to scriptural precepts).

Verses 19–21 say, "Now the works of the flesh are manifest, which are these; Adultery, fornication, uncleanness, lasciviousness [lewdness], Idolatry, witchcraft, hatred, variance [disagreement], emulations [rivalries], wrath, strife, seditions [treasons], heresies, envyings, murders, drunkenness, revellings, and such like:"

Verses 22–23 say, "But the fruit of the Spirit is love, joy, peace, longsuffering [patience], Gentleness, goodness, faith, meekness, temperance [self-control]."

Which list would you like to have in your life? I have experienced life on both sides. I lived among the works of the flesh from approximately twenty-five years of age until the age of thirty-nine. That period of my life was joyless and unfulfilling. It was soured by anger and bitterness. At age thirty-nine, I started to serve God according to biblical principles. It was very difficult at first. As hard as I tried to improve, I still dragged the baggage of sinful habits with me for a long time. Also, I was just beginning to learn biblical principles and how to apply them. As months gave way to years, life got substantially better. As I serve God today, my life is still not perfect, but I can honestly say that it is permeated with the blessings known as the fruit of the Spirit. Anger and bitterness are gone. The quality of my life is much better than when I was sowing to the flesh.

BECAUSE IT LESSENS THE SEVERITY OF GOD'S CHASTENING

Some people object to the teaching that eternal salvation is free, claiming that it leads to a license to sin. Not so. Although God will never abandon believers to hell, He will chasten us to bring us back into line when we are disobedient. Hebrews 12:6 says, "For whom the Lord loveth he chasteneth, and scourgeth every son whom he receiveth."

Chastening is not a bad thing. In fact, it is for our good. Hebrews 12:11 says, "Afterward it yieldeth the peaceable fruit of righteousness unto them which are exercised thereby." However, the weight of God's hand upon us is proportional to our obedience as children. If we are disobedient, it can be heavy indeed. For example, there were some Corinthian believers who were partaking of the Lord's Supper in a casual way, not discerning the Lord's body. Of these people, Paul wrote, "For this cause many are weak and sickly among you, and many sleep [are dead]" (1 Corinthians 11:30).

We should learn from this example. If we are obedient, we can expect the Lord's chastening to be less severe.

BECAUSE IT ACCUMULATES TREASURE IN HEAVEN

I once saw a bumper sticker that caught my attention. It said, "He who dies with the most toys wins." I suppose the owner of the sticker meant it to be humorous, but I was struck by how poignantly it testified to the futility of accumulating possessions in this life.

God has a better plan for us. When we serve Him here on earth, He bestows rewards on us in heaven (1 Corinthians 3:11–15). Jesus said, "Lay not up for yourselves treasures upon earth, where moth and rust doth corrupt, and where thieves break through and steal: But lay up for yourselves treasures in heaven, where neither moth nor rust doth corrupt, and where thieves do not break through nor steal" (Matthew 6:19–20).

Where is your treasure?

CHAPTER FOUR

Fundamentals of the Christian Life

INTRODUCTION

The fundamentals I want to share with you in this chapter are not mine originally, and I don't know where I first heard them. But they have been taught at Calvary Community Church for years, and they have helped me in my spiritual development. I am including them in this book in hopes that they will benefit you in your own walk with the Lord.

PRAYER

Prayer is a powerful resource. It is the means by which we can gain access to the ear of the Almighty God. And He is able to accomplish feats that we cannot even imagine. We never encounter an automated message directing us to enter our date of birth to verify our identity, or instructing us to leave a voicemail. Instead, we are invited to "come boldly unto the throne of grace, that we may obtain mercy, and find grace to help in time of need" (Hebrews 4:16). James 5:16 tells us, "The effectual fervent prayer of a righteous man availeth much."

Through the years, the Lord has blessed me with innumerable answers to prayer. Some were minor, like the time I needed a parking space. Some were more spectacular, like the time a hurricane was bearing down on us. The weather service showed the forecast track coming right through our town. I prayed earnestly. The hurricane diverted just before it reached our area. And then there was the time my wife, Nancy, had a cardiac arrest in my daughter's front yard. I prayed hard and started CPR. Even when the paramedics took over, they could not get her heart started.

I prayed with all my might. They finally did revive her. She recovered, and so far, she has lived thirty-one years after that. There have been many other answers just as wonderful as these.

But what about the times when we pray earnestly and nothing happens? How can we explain that?

There are two reasons given in scripture why the Lord will not hear our prayers. The first is when we harbor unconfessed sin in our hearts. Psalm 66:18 says, "If I regard iniquity in my heart, the Lord will not hear me." The remedy for that is to confess our sins and get back into fellowship with the Lord (1 John 1:9).

The second reason is that our request is not in line with the Lord's will. First John 5:14 says, "And this is the confidence that we have in him, that, if we ask any thing according to his will, he heareth us." Our prayers are answered only if we ask for things that are in accord with God's will. If I ask the Lord to help me rob the convenience store down the street, He will not hear me. The reason is that robbery is not in line with His will (Ephesians 4:28).

BIBLE STUDY

God speaks to us through His scriptures. One of our pastors, Dr. Ralph "Yankee" Arnold, often says, "You cannot know the will of God without knowing the Word of God." The Bible gives us all the information we need to be able to serve the Lord and to be unashamed of our labor. The apostle Paul wrote to Timothy: "All scripture is given by inspiration of God, and is profitable for doctrine, for reproof, for correction, for instruction in righteousness: That the man of God may be perfect, throughly furnished unto all good works" (2 Timothy 3:16–17). "Study to shew thyself approved unto God, a workman that needeth not to be ashamed, rightly dividing the word of truth" (2 Timothy 2:15).

However, a person can actually deceive himself if he does not apply the Word of God by doing what it says. Therefore, it is important to be "doers of the word, and not hearers only" (James 1:22).

Some passages of scripture are easy to understand. Some are difficult. Peter wrote, "And account that the longsuffering of our Lord is salvation; even as our beloved brother Paul also according to the wisdom given unto him hath written unto you; As also in all his epistles, speaking in them of these things; in which are some things hard to be understood, which they that are unlearned and unstable wrest, as they do also the other scriptures, unto their own destruction" (2 Peter 3:15–16).

A rule that has helped me is to never interpret a difficult passage in a way that contradicts one that is plain. Nevertheless, very early in my studies, I felt the need to enlist the help of a faithful Bible teacher. I prayed long and hard for such a teacher. Praise the Lord, He answered my prayers, and that made all the difference.

I encourage you to seek the aid of a faithful teacher if you feel the need. But be diligent. There are many false teachers in the world. The apostle John wrote, "Beloved, believe not every spirit, but try the spirits whether they are of God: because many false prophets are gone out into the world" (1 John 4:1). And these false teachers can be very subtle in their deceitfulness. Paul wrote, "But I fear, lest by any means, as the serpent beguiled Eve through his subtilty, so your minds should be corrupted from the simplicity that is in Christ" (2 Corinthians 11:3).

One might look for a faithful teacher by looking for a good church. Some churches publish their statements of faith online. You can compare their statement of the gospel with the principles laid out in chapter 2 of this book. If a church is clear on the gospel, it is likely that it has some good Bible teachers among its leaders.

You may ask, "What translation should I use?" I use the King James Version (KJV) because the translators aimed at translating the text word for word into English. And I have come to love it. But the KJV uses words common in the seventeenth century, like "thee" and "thou." If you want a good translation that avoids the "thees" and "thous," the New King James Version (NKJV) is an alternative.

CHURCH ATTENDANCE

Regular church attendance is a mandate of scripture. The apostle Paul, who is traditionally believed to be the writer of the book of Hebrews, says, "Not forsaking the assembling of ourselves together, as the manner of some is, but exhorting one another: and so much the more, as ye see the day approaching" (Hebrews 10:25).

There are many benefits to church attendance. For one thing, it is where we can hear the Word of God taught on a regular basis. It is also where we can join together with other believers in the work of proclaiming the gospel to the world, by supporting missionaries and through other evangelical activities. In church, we can also encourage each other in the faith. And it is where we can participate in the keeping of the two ordinances that the Lord left us: water baptism by immersion and the Lord's Supper (communion). Of course, these ordinances are not required of us to receive the free gift of eternal life, but they are symbolic of our faith in Jesus (baptism) and in showing the Lord's death until He comes again (communion).

Finding the right church requires prayer and diligence on your part. Look for a church that publishes its statement of faith online and compare its account of the gospel with the principles laid out in chapter 2 of this book. If the church is not clear on the gospel, avoid it and look somewhere else.

PROCLAIMING THE GOSPEL

When terrorists slammed airliners into the World Trade Center, some people were trapped on floors above the flames. As the flames closed in on them, they became so desperate to escape the pain of death by fire that many of them dove out of windows, plunging to their death on the pavement below. How awful it must have been to be confronted with the prospect of being consumed by fire!

Now imagine a situation where a person is being engulfed in flames with no way to escape, ever. That's the condition of people in hell. Now imagine that you have the power in your hands to save them from that fate. You do. That power is the gospel. What are you willing to do to exercise that power to save people from hell? Hopefully, you care enough to get involved. Paul wrote, "But as we were allowed of God to be put in trust with the gospel, even so we speak, not as pleasing men, but God, which trieth our hearts" (1 Thessalonians 2:4).

How can you get involved? Arm yourself by learning the principles of the gospel spelled out in chapter 2 of this book. Then seek out a church where that gospel is being proclaimed faithfully (see above) and join them in their work. Find tracts that present the gospel faithfully and clearly and share them. Pray for your family members and loved ones and seek opportunities to explain how they can have eternal life as a gift. May the Lord bless you in your endeavors.

BIBLIOGRAPHY

Anderson, Sir Robert. *The Coming Prince.* Grand Rapids: Kregel Classics, 1957.

Bing, Charles C. *Lordship Salvation: A Biblical Evaluation and Response.* USA: Xulon Press, 2010.

Hershey, Doug. *Israel Rising.* New York: Kensington Publishing Corp., 2018.

Hixson, Whitmire, and Roy B. Zuck, ed. *Freely By His Grace: Classical Grace Theology.* Duluth: Grace Gospel Press, 2012.

McClain, Alva J. *Daniel's Prophecy of the 70 Weeks.* Winona Lake: BMH Books, 2007.

McDowell, Josh. *The New Evidence That Demands a Verdict.* Nashville: Thomas Nelson Publishers, 1999.

Pentecost, J. Dwight. "Daniel" In *The Bible Knowledge Commentary: Old Testament*, edited by John F. Walvoord and Roy B. Zuck,1323-1375. USA: Victor Books, 1988.

Stoner, Peter W. *Science Speaks*. Chicago: Moody Press, 1963.

Walvoord, John F. *Every Prophecy of the Bible*. Colorado Springs: David C. Cook, 1990.

Walvoord, John F. *Major Bible Prophecies*. Grand Rapids: Zondervan, 1991.

Printed in the United States
by Baker & Taylor Publisher Services